THE GREATEST PLAYERS

NASCAR

Megan Kopp

MEDIA ENHANCED BOOKS

AV2 BY WEIGL

ADDED VALUE • AUDIO VISUAL

www.av2books.com

MEDIA ENHANCED BOOKS

AV²
BY WEIGL™

ADDED VALUE • AUDIO VISUAL

AV² provides enriched content that supplements and complements this book. Weigl's AV² books strive to create inspired learning and engage young minds in a total learning experience.

Your AV² Media Enhanced books come alive with...

Audio
Listen to sections of the book read aloud.

Video
Watch informative video clips.

Embedded Weblinks
Gain additional information for research.

Key Words
Study vocabulary, and complete a matching word activity.

Quizzes
Test your knowledge.

Slide Show
View images and captions, and prepare a presentation.

Try This!
Complete activities and hands-on experiments.

... and much, much more!

Go to **www.av2books.com**, and enter this book's unique code.

BOOK CODE

J966438

AV² by Weigl brings you media enhanced books that support active learning.

Published by AV² by Weigl
350 5ᵗʰ Avenue, 59ᵗʰ Floor
New York, NY 10118
Website: www.av2books.com   www.weigl.com

Library of Congress Cataloging-in-Publication Data
Kopp, Megan.
 NASCAR / Megan Kopp.
   p. cm. -- (The greatest players)
Includes index.
ISBN 978-1-62127-503-9 (hardcover : alk. paper) -- ISBN 978-1-62127-506-0 (softcover : alk. paper)
1. Stock car drivers--Biography--Juvenile literature. 2. NASCAR (Association)--Juvenile literature. I. Title.
GV1032.A1K66 2013
796.72--dc23
                        2012044835

Printed in the United States of America in North Mankato, Minnesota
1 2 3 4 5 6 7 8 9 0 17 16 15 14 13

032013
WEP300113

Project Coordinator Aaron Carr
Editor Steve Macleod
Art Director Terry Paulhus

Photo Credits
Every reasonable effort has been made to trace ownership and to obtain permission to reprint copyright material. The publishers would be pleased to have any errors or omissions brought to their attention so that they may be corrected in subsequent printings.

Weigl acknowledges Getty Images as its primary image supplier for this title.

Contents

Introduction

The world of professional sports has a long history of great moments. The most memorable moments often come when the sport's greatest players overcome challenging obstacles. For the fans, these moments come to define their favorite sport. For the players, they stand as measuring posts of success.

In 1947, William France Sr. wanted to turn **stock car** racing into an organized sport. He created the **National Association for Stock Car Auto Racing (NASCAR)**. There have been many great drivers and great moments during the sport's history. These include Richard Petty's record 200 wins and Jeff Gordon becoming the youngest driver to win the **Daytona 500** when he was 25. NASCAR has had many of these moments, when the sport's brightest stars accomplished feats that ensured they would be remembered as the greatest drivers.

Driver's Seat

The NASCAR **Sprint Cup Series** has 36 races each year. There are 43 drivers in each race. Drivers earn points based on the place they finish a race. The winning driver receives 43 points. The driver in 43rd place receives one point. Bonus points are also awarded to drivers who are in the lead during the race.

Twelve drivers compete in **The Chase** to win the Sprint Cup Series. The 10 drivers with the most points after 26 races compete in The Chase. The two drivers in the top 20 with the most wins after 26 races also compete in The Chase. The driver who earns the most points during the last 10 races of the season becomes the Sprint Cup Series champion.

Brad Keselowski was the NASCAR Cup Series champion in 2012.

The Racetrack

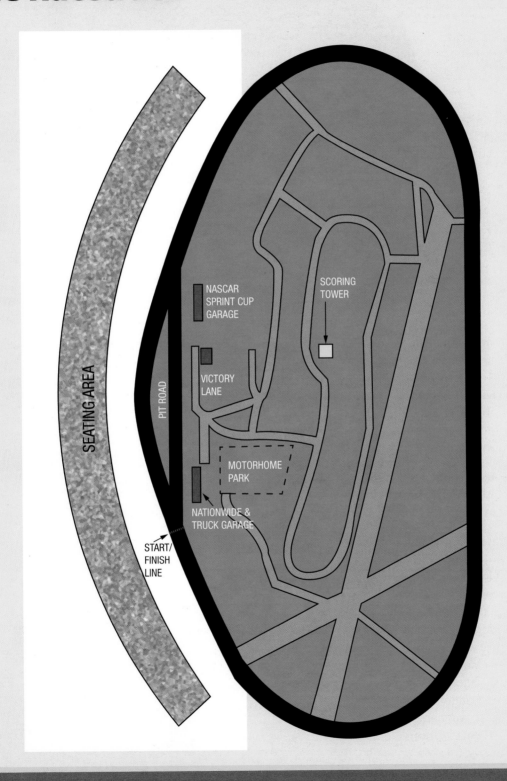

SEATING AREA

PIT ROAD

NASCAR SPRINT CUP GARAGE

VICTORY LANE

MOTORHOME PARK

NATIONWIDE & TRUCK GARAGE

START/ FINISH LINE

SCORING TOWER

> **"Just remember... my grandstand is bigger than your grandstand."**
>
> Bobby Allison

Player Profile

BORN Bobby Allison was born on December 3, 1937, in Miami, Florida.

FAMILY Allison was born to Edmond and Katherine Allison. He was the fourth of 10 children. Allison and his wife Judy were married on February 20, 1960. They had two sons, Davey and Clifford, and two daughters, Bonnie and Carrie.

EDUCATION Allison graduated from Miami's Archbishop Curley Notre Dame High School in 1955.

AWARDS Allison was the **IROC Series** champion in 1980. He won the NASCAR Cup Series in 1983 and was named NASCAR's Most Popular Driver in 1971, 1972, 1973, 1981, 1982, and 1983. He won the NASCAR Award of Excellence in 1989. He was inducted into the International Motorsports Hall of Fame and the National Motorsports Press Association's Hall of Fame in 1993. Allison was named one of NASCAR's 50 Greatest Drivers in 1998. He was inducted into the NASCAR Hall of Fame in 2011.

Bobby Allison's sons Davey and Clifford both became race car drivers. Tragically, Clifford died when his race car crashed in 1992. Davey died in a helicopter crash one year later.

Bobby Allison
NASCAR #12

Early Years

Bobby Allison started racing cars during his senior year of high school. He finished in 10th place in his first race. Allison's father made him stop racing after he got into a few crashes. After Allison graduated from high school, he got a job testing boat engines. He then became a NASCAR mechanic. These jobs taught Allison how to keep a car running at its best.

Allison took a trip to Alabama in 1959 with his brother Donnie and two friends. Allison drove in three car races during their trip. He finished in fifth place in one race and second place in another race. Two weeks later, they went back to Alabama. Allison won a race after starting in last place. It was his first victory. Allison soon moved to Alabama. His brother Donnie and his racing hero Red Farmer moved with him. They won many races and became known as the Alabama Gang.

Developing Skills

Allison raced **modified stock cars**. He won NASCAR modified stock car championships from 1962 to 1965. Allison won his first NASCAR Cup Series race in 1966 at the Oxford Plains Speedway in Maine. He won his first Daytona 500 in 1978.

Allison was the NASCAR Cup Series champion in 1983. He won six races that year. He also finished in the top 10 in 25 races during 1983. Allison placed second in the Cup Series five times. During his career, he won 84 NASCAR races. He is tied for fourth in career race wins with Darrell Waltrip. Allison was forced to retire from racing in 1988 after a serious accident at a racetrack in Pennsylvania.

Bobby Allison

Greatest Moment

Allison led the Daytona 500 for 147 laps in 1982. He beat Cale Yarborough to the finish line by 22.87 seconds. It was the second time Allison won the Daytona 500. He earned $120,630 for the victory. Allison became the first driver to win more than $100,000 from a Cup Series race.

Allison was 50 years old during the Daytona 500 in 1988. He won the race and crossed the finish line one car length ahead of his son Davey. It was the first time a father and son finished in first and second place.

Bobby Allison earned more than $7.5 million from racing events during his career.

"The winner ain't the one with the fastest car; it's the one who refuses to lose."

Dale Earnhardt

Dale Earnhardt was nicknamed "The Intimidator" because of his aggressive driving style.

Player Profile

BORN Ralph Dale Earnhardt was born on April 29, 1951, in Kannapolis, North Carolina.

FAMILY Earnhardt was born to Ralph Earnhardt and Martha King. He had four siblings. Earnhardt was married three times and had four children: Kerry, Kelley, Dale Jr., and Taylor.

EDUCATION Earnhardt did not finish high school.

AWARDS Earnhardt was NASCAR Rookie of the Year in 1979. He was the NASCAR Cup Series champion in 1980, 1986, 1987, 1990, 1991, 1993, and 1994. Earnhardt won the National Motorsports Press Association's Driver of the Year award in 1980, 1986, 1987, 1990, and 1994. He was named one of NASCAR's 50 Greatest Drivers in 1998. He was inducted into the NASCAR Hall of Fame in 2010.

Dale Earnhardt

NASCAR #2

Early Years

Dale Earnhardt's father, Ralph, was a well-known race car driver. He won many **short-track** events in North Carolina. He was the NASCAR Sportsman Division champion in 1956. Ralph Earnhardt died of a heart attack on September 26, 1973. It happened while he was working on his car at a racetrack.

Earnhardt wanted to race like his father. He started racing at local tracks when he was 15. He left school in the ninth grade to work as a mechanic and race cars. Earnhardt competed in his first NASCAR Cup Series race in 1975. It was the World 600 at the Charlotte Motor Speedway. He finished in 22nd place.

Developing Skills

Earnhardt won his first NASCAR Cup Series race in 1979. He raced in 27 Cup Series events that year. He finished in the top five in 11 of those races. Earnhardt finished the season in seventh place. He was named Rookie of the Year in 1979.

Earnhardt was the Cup Series champion for the first time in 1980. That year, he won five races and finished in the top 10 in 24 races. Earnhardt raced in 676 Cup Series events during his career. He finished in the top 10 in 428 races and won 76 Cup Series events. This is the seventh most wins by a driver in NASCAR history. In 2001, Earnhardt crashed during the final lap of the Daytona 500. He died from his injuries. Earnhardt was 49 years old.

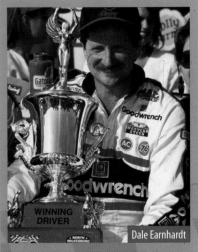

Dale Earnhardt

Greatest Moment

Earnhardt won his first Daytona 500 in 1998. It was his 20th attempt to win the race. He had finished second at the event four times. Earnhardt was in first place for 107 of the race's 200 laps, and he beat Bobby Labonte across the finish line. Crew members from every racing team lined up in the **pit** after the race. They all congratulated Earnhardt on the victory.

In 1996, Dale Earnhardt became the first driver to start in 500 consecutive Cup Series races.

> **"I want to force the other drivers to find a way past me."**
>
> Jeff Gordon

Jeff Gordon set a NASCAR record in 1999 by finishing in the top 10 in 21 straight races.

Player Profile

BORN Jeffrey Michael Gordon was born on August 4, 1971, in Vallejo, California.

FAMILY Gordon was born to Will and Carol Gordon. He has a sister named Kimberly. Gordon married Ingrid Vandebosch in 2006. The couple has a daughter named Ella Sofia and a son named Leo Benjamin.

EDUCATION Gordon graduated from Tri-West High School in Indiana in 1989.

AWARDS Gordon was the NASCAR Cup Series Rookie of the Year in 1993. He won the NASCAR Cup Series in 1995, 1997, 1998, and 2001. He was named the National Motorsports Press Association's Driver of the Year in 1995 and 1998. He was named one of NASCAR's 50 Greatest Drivers in 1998.

Jeff Gordon

NASCAR #24

Early Years

Jeff Gordon's parents divorced shortly after he was born. His stepfather John Bickford built a racetrack at an old fairground, and Gordon started racing when he was 5 years old. He competed in **quarter midget** events. Gordon's second year of racing was in 1978. He won 35 main events that year. He also set speed records at five different racetracks. The next year, he competed in races around the country. He won the quarter midget Grand National Championship in Denver.

Gordon started racing bigger cars as he got older. He competed in his first **sprint car** race at age 13. Gordon's family moved to Indianapolis in 1986. This allowed him to compete in more sprint car races. Gordon raced in the United States Auto Club midget series in 1989. He was named Rookie of the Year that year. He was the midget series champion in 1990.

Developing Skills

Gordon spent two years racing in the NASCAR Grand National Series. It is now called the **Nationwide Series**. He was named Rookie of the Year for that series in 1991. He finished fourth in the series in 1992. That year, he also raced in one event in the NASCAR Cup Series. The race was at the Atlanta Motor Speedway. Gordon crashed and did not finish the race. In 1993, Gordon raced in all 30 events of the NASCAR Cup Series. He finished in the top 10 in 11 of those races. He finished the season in 14th place and was named Rookie of the Year.

Gordon won his first NASCAR Cup Series race in 1994. He beat Rusty Wallace by 3.91 seconds at the Coca-Cola 600. Gordon has 87 career Cup Series wins. This is the third most wins in NASCAR history.

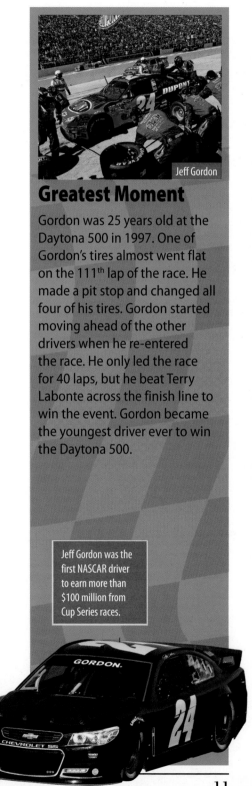

Jeff Gordon

Greatest Moment

Gordon was 25 years old at the Daytona 500 in 1997. One of Gordon's tires almost went flat on the 111th lap of the race. He made a pit stop and changed all four of his tires. Gordon started moving ahead of the other drivers when he re-entered the race. He only led the race for 40 laps, but he beat Terry Labonte across the finish line to win the event. Gordon became the youngest driver ever to win the Daytona 500.

Jeff Gordon was the first NASCAR driver to earn more than $100 million from Cup Series races.

"You always think you've got enough ability to win, but you never know until you get out there and do it."

Jimmie Johnson

Jimmie Johnson has finished in the top 10 every year since he started racing in the NASCAR Cup Series in 2002.

Player Profile

BORN Jimmie Johnson was born on September 17, 1975, in El Cajon, California.

FAMILY Johnson was born to Gary and Cathy Johnson. He has two younger brothers named Jarit and Jessie. Johnson married Chandra Janway in 2004. The couple has a daughter named Genevieve Marie.

EDUCATION Johnson graduated from Granite Hills High School in El Cajon, California, in 1993.

AWARDS Johnson won the NASCAR Cup Series in 2006, 2007, 2008, 2009, and 2010. He won the ESPY Award for Best Driver in 2008, 2009, 2010, and 2011.

Jimmie Johnson
NASCAR #48

Early Years

Jimmie Johnson started riding motorcycles when he was 4 years old. He started competing in **motocross** races at age 5. When he was 8, Johnson broke his knee. He had a cast on his leg for the final race of the season. He won his first series championship that year. Johnson competed in races around the country during high school. He won the motocross stadium championship in 1992.

Johnson started **off-road racing** in 1993. He won the SCORE Desert Series title in 1994. He also won off-road winter championships in 1996 and 1997. In 1998, Johnson started stock car racing in the NASCAR Grand National Series. In his first race, he finished in 25th place.

Developing Skills

Johnson's first full year in the Grand National Division was in 2000. He finished in the top 10 in six races and ended the year in 10th place. Johnson joined the NASCAR Cup Series in 2002. He won his first Cup Series race during his rookie season. It was the NAPA Auto Parts 500 at the California Speedway. That year, he finished in the top 10 in 21 races. He finished the season in fifth place.

Johnson won 60 events in his first 11 years racing in the Cup Series. This is the eighth most wins in NASCAR history. Johnson won the Cup Series for the first time in 2006. He was also the Cup Series champion the next four years in a row. He is the first driver ever to win the Cup Series in five straight years.

Jimmie Johnson

Greatest Moment

Johnson's motocross **idol** was Rick Johnson. They are not related. When Johnson was 7 years old, Rick came to one of his races. Johnson wanted to impress his hero. He used a six-foot (1.8 meter) jump and sailed 65 feet (20 m) through the air. He made a perfect landing. Rick was impressed. He later introduced Johnson to car racing.

In 2009, Jimmie Johnson became the first race car driver ever to be named the Associated Press Male Athlete of the Year.

> "They were pushing everything to the limit, using special grease in the wheel bearings and things like that — stuff you wouldn't really need today, but you did then."
>
> David Pearson

David Pearson was nicknamed the "Silver Fox" because of his crafty and patient driving.

Player Profile

BORN David Gene Pearson was born on December 22, 1934, in Whitney, South Carolina.

FAMILY Pearson was born to Eura and Lennie Pearson. He was the youngest of three children. Pearson's wife, Helen, died in 1991. They had three sons: Larry, Ricky, and Eddie.

EDUCATION Pearson left high school when he was 16.

AWARDS Pearson was named NASCAR Rookie of the Year in 1960. He won the NASCAR Cup Series in 1966, 1968, and 1969. He was named the National Motorsports Press Association's Driver of the Year in 1973. He was inducted into the International Motorsports Hall of Fame in 1991 and into the National Motorsports Press Association's Hall of Fame in 1995. Pearson was named one of NASCAR's 50 Greatest Drivers in 1998. He was inducted into the NASCAR Hall of Fame in 2011.

David Pearson
NASCAR #21

Early Years

David Pearson climbed a tree when he was a child to watch stock car races at the fairgrounds in Spartanburg, South Carolina. He started racing in local short-track events in 1952. Pearson was 17 years old, and he won $13 in his first race.

In 1959, Pearson won the track championship at the Greenville-Pickens Speedway in South Carolina. The next year, he joined the NASCAR Cup Series. Pearson drove in 22 races during his first season. He did not win a race that year, but he did finish in the top 10 in seven races. Pearson ended the season in 23rd place and was named NASCAR Rookie of the Year in 1960.

Developing Skills

Pearson won his first NASCAR Cup Series race in 1961. He won the World 600 at the Charlotte Motor Speedway by two laps. He also won two other races during 1961 and finished the year in 13th place. In 1964, Pearson raced in 61 of 62 Cup Series events. He won eight of those races and finished in the top 10 in 42 races. He ended the season in third place.

Pearson raced in 42 of the 49 events in 1966. He won 15 races and finished in the top 10 in 33 races. That year, he won his first NASCAR Cup Series championship. Pearson only missed one race when he won the Cup Series in 1968. He missed three races when he won the Cup Series in 1969. Pearson competed in 574 events during 27 years of racing in the NASCAR Cup Series. He finished in the top 10 in 366 races. He won 105 races. It is the second most wins in NASCAR history.

David Pearson

Greatest Moment

The Daytona 500 in 1976 was a duel between Pearson and Richard Petty. The two drivers took turns leading the race during the last 20 laps. Petty had the lead going into the final lap. The two cars bumped into each other on the fourth turn. Both cars slid onto the grass **infield**. Petty's engine stalled, but Pearson managed to drive his damaged car across the finish line. It was his first Daytona 500 victory.

In 1969, David Pearson reached a speed of 190.029 miles (278.7 kilometers) per hour during the qualifying laps of the Daytona 500. He became the first driver to go faster than 190 miles per hour at the Daytona International Speedway.

"I figure you get out of life just about what you put into it."

Lee Petty

Lee Petty created a racing team called Petty Enterprises. Between 1949 and 2008, drivers with Petty Enterprises won 268 races and 11 NASCAR Cup Series championships.

Player Profile

BORN Lee Arnold Petty was born on March 14, 1914, in Randleman, North Carolina.

FAMILY Petty was born to Judson and Jessie Petty. He married Elizabeth Toomes in 1936. The couple had two sons, Richard and Maurice.

EDUCATION Petty attended King's Business College in North Carolina.

AWARDS Petty was the NASCAR Cup Series champion in 1954, 1958, and 1959. He was inducted into the International Motorsports Hall of Fame in 1990. He was named one of NASCAR's 50 Greatest Drivers in 1998. He was inducted into the NASCAR Hall of Fame in 2011.

Lee Petty
NASCAR #42

Early Years

Lee Petty worked as a truck driver. He also worked on cars for drivers who raced on dirt roads around North Carolina. Petty and his brother decided to enter a car in an organized race at an oval track. They won their first race. Stock car racing was not an organized sport yet, so Petty continued to work full-time and watch local races.

In 1948, Petty traveled with his two sons to Daytona, Florida, to watch stock car racing. Petty met NASCAR founder William France Sr. at the event. Petty joined the NASCAR Cup Series the next year. He was 35 years old. The first race that season was at the Charlotte Speedway. Petty crashed after completing 105 laps. He did not finish the race.

Developing Skills

Petty won his first NASCAR Cup Series race in October 1949 at the Heidelberg Raceway in Pittsburgh, Pennsylvania. It was Petty's fifth NASCAR race. Petty raced in six of the eight NASCAR events held in 1949. He finished in the top 10 in five races. He finished the season in second place.

Petty won the NASCAR Cup Series for the first time in 1954. He won the Cup Series again in 1958 and 1959. He was the first driver to win the Cup Series three times. Petty finished in the top six each season during his first 12 years of racing in the NASCAR Cup Series. Petty entered 427 NASCAR races during his career. He finished in the top 10 in 332 of those races. Petty won 54 races. This is the 10th most wins in the history of NASCAR.

Lee Petty

Greatest Moment

The first Daytona 500 at the brand new Daytona International Speedway was held on February 22, 1959. Petty and Johnny Beauchamp exchanged leads in the final laps of the race. Joe Weatherly caught up with them at the final turn, and the three drivers crossed the finish line at the same time. Officials at the race awarded the victory to Beauchamp. After looking at photos and watching replays of the finish for almost three days, officials declared Petty the winner.

Lee Petty started a racing tradition. His son Richard, grandson Kyle, and great-grandson Adam have all competed in NASCAR Cup Series races. The Petty's are the only family to have four different generations race in NASCAR events.

> "No one wants to quit when he's losing and no one wants to quit when he's winning."

Richard Petty

Player Profile

BORN Richard Lee Petty was born on July 2, 1937, in Level Cross, North Carolina.

FAMILY Petty was born to Lee and Elizabeth Petty. He has a brother named Maurice. Petty married Lynda Owens in 1959. They have four children: Kyle, Sharon, Lisa, and Rebecca.

EDUCATION Petty graduated from Randleman High School in 1955. He attended King's Business College in North Carolina.

AWARDS Petty was named NASCAR Rookie of the Year in 1959. He won the NASCAR Cup Series in 1964, 1967, 1971, 1972, 1974, 1975, and 1979. He was named the National Motorsports Press Association's Driver of the Year in 1974 and 1975. He was inducted into the International Motorsports Hall of Fame in 1997. He was named one of NASCAR's 50 Greatest Drivers in 1998. He was inducted into the NASCAR Hall of Fame in 2010.

Richard Petty is nicknamed "The King" because of all the records he set at the Daytona 500 and other NASCAR races.

Richard Petty
NASCAR #43

Early Years

In 1948, Richard Petty went to his first NASCAR race. He was 11 years old and traveled to Daytona, Florida, with his father and brother for the race. The next year, Petty and his brother Maurice worked as the pit crew for their father's first NASCAR Cup Series race. The two brothers continued working for their father. They helped prepare his cars for races. Petty also wanted to race. His father told him he could not race until he was 21 years old.

Petty entered his first NASCAR race 10 days after he turned 21. The race was part of the **Convertible Series** and was held at the Columbia Speedway in South Carolina. Petty finished in sixth place. The next week, he entered his first NASCAR Cup Series race. The event was in Toronto, Canada. Petty's father was also competing in the same race. During the 55th lap, Petty was in front of his father. Petty's father bumped his car and Petty crashed into the wall. Petty did not finish the race.

Developing Skills

Petty's first season in the NASCAR Cup Series was in 1959. He only raced in 21 of the 44 events that year. He finished in the top 10 in nine of those races and finished the season in 15th place. He was named NASCAR Rookie of the Year. Petty won his first NASCAR Cup Series race in February 1960. He won two other races that year and finished in the top 10 in 30 races. He ended the year in second place.

Petty won his first Daytona 500 race in 1964. He also won his first NASCAR Cup Series championship that year. Petty won the Cup Series again in 1967, 1971, 1972, 1974, 1975, and 1979. He was the first driver to win the Cup Series seven times. Petty raced in the Cup Series for 35 years. He won 200 races, which is the most wins in NASCAR history.

Richard Petty

Greatest Moment

In 1967, Petty won the Wilkes 400 at the North Wilkesboro Speedway in North Carolina by two laps. It was his 27th victory of the season. It was also his 10th win in a row. Both of these feats were NASCAR records.

Bobby Allison was leading the Daytona 500 in 1981. He made a pit stop during the 173rd lap for fuel and new tires. Petty stopped for just fuel. He took the lead when he left the pit ahead of Allison. Petty only led the race for 26 laps, but he beat Allison to the finish line by 3.5 seconds. It was Petty's seventh win at the Daytona 500. He won the race more times than any other driver in history.

The National Motorsports Press Association's annual award for the best driver is named the Richard Petty Driver of the Year award.

> "I think any older driver would find it different than it was five years ago."

Darrell Waltrip

Darrell Waltrip now works as a NASCAR analyst on television for Fox Sports.

Player Profile

BORN Darrell Waltrip was born on February 5, 1947, in Owensboro, Kentucky.

FAMILY Margaret and Leroy Waltrip raised five children: Darrell, Michael, Bobby, Carolyn, and Connie. Waltrip married Stephanie Rader in 1969. The couple has two daughters, Jessica and Sarah.

EDUCATION Waltrip graduated from Daviess County High School in Owensboro, Kentucky, in 1965.

AWARDS Waltrip was the NASCAR Cup Series champion in 1981, 1982, and 1985. He was named the National Motorsports Press Association's Driver of the Year in 1976, 1981, and 1982. He was inducted into the International Motorsports Hall of Fame in 2005. Waltrip was named one of NASCAR's 50 Greatest Drivers in 1998. He was inducted into the NASCAR Hall of Fame in 2012.

Darrell Waltrip
NASCAR #17

Early Years

Darrell Waltrip started his racing career when he was 12 years old. His father bought him a go-kart. Waltrip started competing in go-kart races on weekends. He won the first race he entered. When he turned 16, Waltrip started racing cars in short-track races.

Waltrip entered his first NASCAR Cup Series race at age 25. It was the 1972 Winston 500 at the Alabama International Motor Speedway in Talladega, Alabama. He only completed 69 laps of the race. Waltrip raced in five NASCAR Cup Series events that year. He finished in the top 10 in three of those races.

Developing Skills

Waltrip won his first NASCAR Cup Series race in the Music City USA 420 at the Nashville Speedway in 1975. He won two races that season and finished in the top 10 in 11 races. He finished the season in seventh place. Waltrip finished in the top 10 in the NASCAR Cup Series every year for the next 14 seasons.

Waltrip won 12 races in 1981. He won his first NASCAR Cup Series championship that year. The next year, he won 12 races for his second NASCAR Cup Series title. In 1985, Waltrip only won three races, but he finished in the top 10 in 21 of the 28 events. He earned enough points to win his third Cup Series championship. Waltrip raced in the NASCAR Cup Series for 29 years. He won 84 races. He is tied with Bobby Allison for the fourth most wins in NASCAR history.

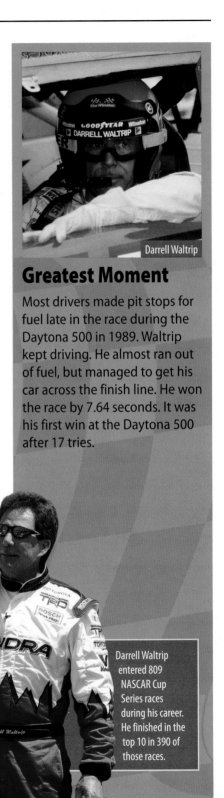

Darrell Waltrip

Greatest Moment

Most drivers made pit stops for fuel late in the race during the Daytona 500 in 1989. Waltrip kept driving. He almost ran out of fuel, but managed to get his car across the finish line. He won the race by 7.64 seconds. It was his first win at the Daytona 500 after 17 tries.

Darrell Waltrip entered 809 NASCAR Cup Series races during his career. He finished in the top 10 in 390 of those races.

> "I feel like I got a pile of cattle chasing (me), and I'm pedaling as hard as I can to stay in front of 'em."

Rusty Wallace

Player Profile

BORN Russell William Wallace, Jr. was born on August 14, 1956, in St. Louis, Missouri.

FAMILY Wallace was born to Russ and Judy Wallace. He has two brothers, Kenny and Mike. Wallace and his wife Patti have three children: Greg, Katie, and Steve.

EDUCATION Wallace graduated from Fox High School in Arnold, Missouri.

AWARDS Wallace was the NASCAR Rookie of the Year in 1984. He was the NASCAR Cup Series champion in 1989. He was named the National Motorsports Press Association's Driver of the Year in 1988 and 1993. Wallace was named one of NASCAR's 50 Greatest Drivers in 1998. He was inducted into the NASCAR Hall of Fame and the International Motorsports Hall of Fame in 2013.

Rusty Wallace made an appearance as himself in a 1990 movie about stock car racing called *Days of Thunder*.

Rusty Wallace
NASCAR #2

Early Years

Russell Wallace, Sr. worked as a mechanic and later was co-owner of a janitorial supply business. In his spare time, he raced cars at dirt tracks around the St. Louis area. Rusty Wallace and his two brothers helped their dad prepare his cars for racing.

Wallace started racing stock cars in 1973. That year, he was named the Central Racing Association Rookie of the Year. Between 1974 and 1978, he won more than 200 races. In 1979, he was named Rookie of the Year in the United States Auto Club stock car division. Wallace competed in his first NASCAR Cup Series race in 1980. It was in the Atlanta 500 at the Atlanta International Raceway. He finished in second place. Wallace competed in one other Cup Series race that year.

Developing Skills

Wallace's first full season racing in the NASCAR Cup Series was in 1984. He competed in all 30 races that year. Wallace did not win a race, but he finished in the top 10 in four events. He ended the season in 14th place and was named NASCAR Rookie of the Year.

Wallace won his first NASCAR Cup Series race in 1986 at the Bristol International Speedway in Tennessee. He won the NASCAR Cup Series championship in 1989. Wallace raced in the Cup Series for 25 years. He finished in the top 20 in 23 of those seasons. Wallace raced in 706 races during his career. He finished in the top 10 in 349 events and won 55 races. This is the ninth most wins by a driver in NASCAR history.

Rusty Wallace

Greatest Moment

Wallace's friend Alan Kulwicki won the NASCAR Cup Series in 1992. Tragically, Kulwicki died in a plane crash in April 2003. A few days later, Wallace won a race at the Bristol International Speedway. As a tribute to his friend, Wallace drove his victory lap backwards. The "Polish victory lap" was one of Kulwicki's signature moves.

In 1989, Wallace started racing in the IROC Series. He won the event at the Daytona International Speedway on February 17, 1989, after starting the race in last place. It was the first time a driver had won an IROC event after starting in the last position.

Rusty Wallace's son Steve Wallace competed in his first NASCAR Cup Series event at the Daytona 500 in 2011. He finished in 20th place.

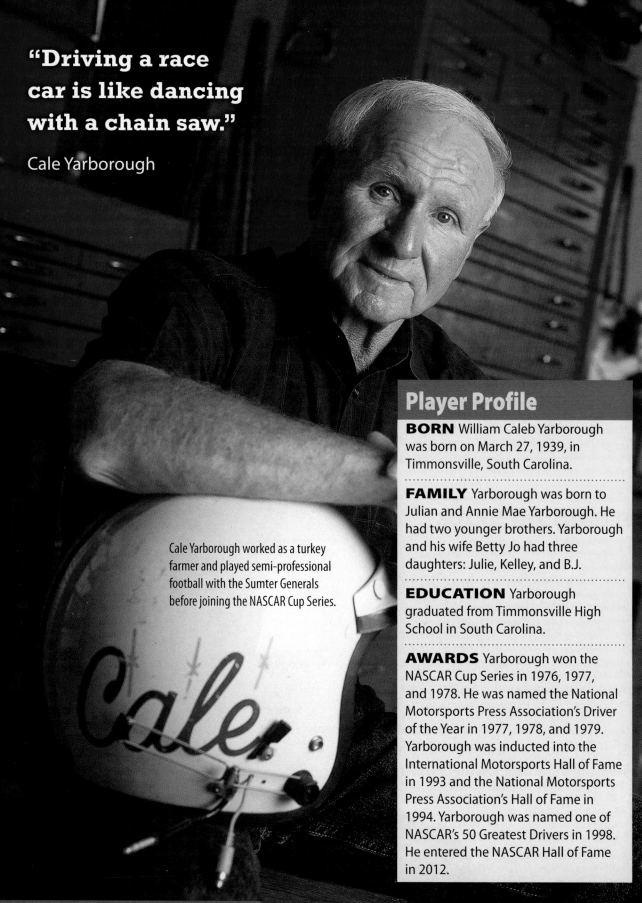

"Driving a race car is like dancing with a chain saw."

Cale Yarborough

Cale Yarborough worked as a turkey farmer and played semi-professional football with the Sumter Generals before joining the NASCAR Cup Series.

Player Profile

BORN William Caleb Yarborough was born on March 27, 1939, in Timmonsville, South Carolina.

FAMILY Yarborough was born to Julian and Annie Mae Yarborough. He had two younger brothers. Yarborough and his wife Betty Jo had three daughters: Julie, Kelley, and B.J.

EDUCATION Yarborough graduated from Timmonsville High School in South Carolina.

AWARDS Yarborough won the NASCAR Cup Series in 1976, 1977, and 1978. He was named the National Motorsports Press Association's Driver of the Year in 1977, 1978, and 1979. Yarborough was inducted into the International Motorsports Hall of Fame in 1993 and the National Motorsports Press Association's Hall of Fame in 1994. Yarborough was named one of NASCAR's 50 Greatest Drivers in 1998. He entered the NASCAR Hall of Fame in 2012.

Cale Yarborough
NASCAR #28

Early Years

Cale Yarborough and his father built a car so that Yarborough could race in a **Soap Box Derby**. He later got his driver's license at age 14 and bought his first car. Yarborough began racing on the rural roads around Timmonsville, South Carolina. In high school, he bought a new car. With help from his friends, Yarborough brought the car to a local dirt track. He finished in third place in his first race.

Yarborough competed in his first NASCAR Cup Series race when he was 18 years old. He was too young to enter the race, but he told the officials he was 21. It was in the 1957 Southern 500 at the Darlington Raceway in South Carolina. He only completed 31 laps before race officials found out his real age and made him stop driving.

Developing Skills

Yarborough competed in one NASCAR Cup Series race each year from 1957 to 1961. He won his first Cup Series race in 1965. It was on a dirt track at the Valdosta Speedway in Georgia. It was his only victory that year. During the season, he raced in 46 of the 55 events. He finished in the top 10 in 21 races. He finished 10th overall in the Cup Series that year.

Yarborough won the NASCAR Cup Series in 1976, 1977, and 1978. He became the first driver to win the championship three times in a row. Yarborough competed in 560 Cup Series races in 31 years. He won 83 races, which is the sixth most career wins in NASCAR history.

Cale Yarborough

Greatest Moment

The Daytona 500 in 1979 was the first NASCAR race to be shown on national television from start to finish. Yarborough and Donnie Allison got into a car crash while competing for the lead during the last lap of the race. The drivers got out of their cars and started arguing. Then a fight broke out on national television.

Yarborough won the Daytona 500 for the fourth time in 1984. During the qualifying laps he became the first driver at Daytona to go faster than 200 miles (293 km) per hour.

Cale Yarborough painted the number 35 on the side of his car in high school. It was the same number he wore on his football jersey.

Greatest Moments

1948
The first official NASCAR race is held at Daytona Beach, Florida, on February 15.

1959
The first Daytona 500 is held. Lee Petty wins the race in a photo finish.

1976 – The Greatest Finish

When: February 15, 1976

Where: Daytona Beach, Florida

In the final lap of the Daytona 500, David Pearson and Richard Petty crash while coming out of turn four. Petty's car will not restart, but Pearson manages to keep his car running and wins the race. He crosses the finish

line at about 10 miles (16 km) per hour. It is the slowest speed ever recorded by a winning driver when crossing the finish line at the Daytona 500.

1940   1950   1960   1970   1980   1985

1977
Janet Guthrie becomes the first woman to ever compete at the Daytona 500. She finishes in 12th place and is the top rookie of the race. That same year she is also the first woman to compete in the Indy 500.

1979
Cale Yarborough and Donnie Allison get into a fight on national television during the Daytona 500.

1985 – The Million Dollar Bill

When: September 1, 1985

Where: Darlington, South Carolina

Bill Elliott wins the Southern 500 to complete the Winston Million. Earlier in the year, he won the Daytona 500 and the Winston 500. He is the first driver to win all three races in one season and earn a $1 million bonus. Jeff Gordon is the only other driver to win the Winston Million.

1987 – The Pass in the Grass

When: May 17, 1987

Where: Concord, North Carolina

Dale Earnhardt is leading Bill Elliott with seven laps left in the race during NASCAR's All-Star event at the Charlotte Motor Speedway. Elliott tries to tuck under Earnhardt's car to take the lead. Earnhardt tries to block Elliott, but he slides onto the grass infield. Earnhardt keeps control of his car and gets back on the racetrack to win the event.

2004
NASCAR introduces The Chase. The new playoff format is used to determine the Cup Series champion.

2010
Jimmie Johnson is the first driver to win the NASCAR Cup Series five years in a row.

1990   **1995**   **2000**   **2005**   **2010**

1988
Bobby and Davey Allison are the first father and son to finish in first and second place at the Daytona 500.

2011 – Three Finger Salute

When: February 20, 2011

Where: Daytona Beach, Florida

It is the 10 year anniversary of Dale Earnhardt's death during the Daytona 500 in 2001. Race officials organize a special tribute for the legendary driver. They ask fans in the stands to remain silent during the third lap of the race and put three fingers in the air to honor Earnhardt, and the number three he had painted on his race car.

Write a Biography

Life Story

A person's life story can be the subject of a book. This kind of book is called a biography. Biographies often describe the lives of people who have achieved great success. These people may be alive today, or they may have lived many years ago. Reading a biography can help you learn more about a great person.

Get the Facts

Use this book, and research in the library and on the Internet, to find out more about your favorite NASCAR driver. Learn as much about this driver as you can. What type of car does this person drive? What are his or her statistics in important categories? Has this person set any records? Also, be sure to write down key events in the person's life. What was this person's childhood like? What has he or she accomplished? Is there anything else that makes this person special or unusual?

Tony Stewart has won 47 NASCAR Cup Series races during his career. He was the Cup Series champion in 2002, 2005, and 2011.

Use the Concept Web

A concept web is a useful research tool. Read the questions in the concept web on the following page. Answer the questions in your notebook. Your answers will help you write a biography.

Concept Web

- What did you learn from the books you read in your research?
- Would you suggest these books to others?
- Was anything missing from these books?

- Where does this individual currently reside?
- Does he or she have a family?

- Where and when was this person born?
- Describe his or her parents, siblings, and friends.
- Did this person grow up in unusual circumstances?

Your Opinion

Adulthood

Childhood

WRITING A BIOGRAPHY

Main Accomplishments

Help and Obstacles

Work and Preparation

- What is this person's life's work?
- Has he or she received awards or recognition for accomplishments?
- How have this person's accomplishments served others?

- Did this individual have a positive attitude?
- Did he or she receive help from others?
- Did this person have a mentor?
- Did this person face any hardships?
- If so, how were the hardships overcome?

- What was this person's education?
- What was his or her work experience?
- How does this person work; what is the process he or she uses?

Know your STUFF!

1 How many drivers compete in The Chase?

2 Who has won more NASCAR Cup Series races than any other driver?

3 Which drivers were called the Alabama Gang?

4 Who was the first driver to win the NASCAR Cup Series five years in a row?

5 What two drivers have won the Winston Million?

6 What two jobs did Cale Yarborough have before joining the NASCAR Cup Series?

7 Who is William France Sr.?

8 How many years did David Pearson compete in every race during a NASCAR Cup Series season?

9 What is the record for most wins during a NASCAR Cup Series season?

10 In what sport did Jimmie Johnson compete at age 5?

ANSWERS: 1. 12 2. Richard Petty 3. Bobby Allison, Donnie Allison, and Red Farmer 4. Jimmie Johnson 5. Bill Elliott and Jeff Gordon 6. A turkey farmer and a semi-professional football player 7. William France Sr. created NASCAR 8. None 9. Richard Petty had 27 wins in 1967 10. Motocross

Key Words

Convertible Series: a group of race events for cars with roofs that can be removed

Daytona 500: a 500-mile (805-km) race that goes for 200 laps at the Daytona International Speedway in Daytona Beach, Florida; it is the first race of the NASCAR season

idol: a greatly admired person

infield: the area in the middle of a racetrack

IROC Series: a group of race events where the top drivers from different types of car racing drive identical cars to determine who is the best driver

modified stock cars: cars that were driven for everyday use but have had many changes made to them to turn them into race cars

motocross: a motorcycle race held on a racetrack built on rough ground, usually dirt

National Association for Stock Car Auto Racing (NASCAR): an organization created to set up race events and make rules for competition

Nationwide Series: a group of stock car race events organized by NASCAR and usually held the day before Cup Series races

off-road racing: races held on courses that are different from typical driving surfaces of pavement or asphalt

pit: an area beside the racetrack used to fuel and repair cars during a race

quarter midget: a small race car designed for children

short-track: a racetrack that is less than 1 mile (1.6 km) in length

Soap Box Derby: an event where children race homemade cars down a hill

sprint car: a race car designed specially to race on a dirt racetrack

Sprint Cup Series: a group of race events organized by NASCAR for the organization's best drivers

stock car: a race car based on a model built at a factory for everyday use, but specially designed to drive only on a racetrack

The Chase: a playoff format created by NASCAR to determine a champion for each Cup Series season

Index

Log on to www.av2books.com

AV² by Weigl brings you media enhanced books that support active learning. Go to www.av2books.com, and enter the special code found on page 2 of this book. You will gain access to enriched and enhanced content that supplements and complements this book. Content includes video, audio, weblinks, quizzes, a slide show, and activities.

AV² Online Navigation

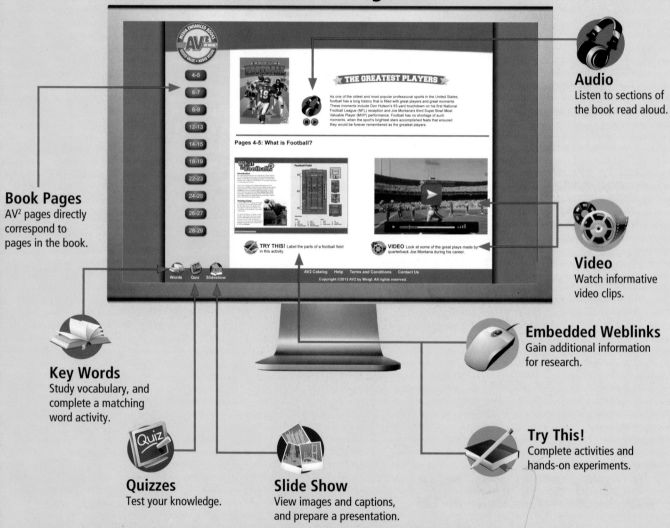

Audio
Listen to sections of the book read aloud.

Book Pages
AV² pages directly correspond to pages in the book.

Video
Watch informative video clips.

Key Words
Study vocabulary, and complete a matching word activity.

Embedded Weblinks
Gain additional information for research.

Try This!
Complete activities and hands-on experiments.

Quizzes
Test your knowledge.

Slide Show
View images and captions, and prepare a presentation.

AV² was built to bridge the gap between print and digital. We encourage you to tell us what you like and what you want to see in the future.

Sign up to be an AV² Ambassador at www.av2books.com/ambassador.